Greater Than a Tourist Book S

I think the series is wonderful and beneficial for tourists to get information before visiting the city.

-Seckin Zumbul, Izmir Turkey

I am a world traveler who has read many trip guides but this one really made a difference for me. I would call it a heartfelt creation of a local guide expert instead of just a guide.

-Susy, Isla Holbox, Mexico

New to the area like me, this is a must have!

-Joe, Bloomington, USA

This is a good series that gets down to it when looking for things to do at your destination without having to read a novel for just a few ideas.

-Rachel, Monterey, USA

Good information to have to plan my trip to this destination.

-Pennie Farrell, Mexico

Aptly titled, you won't just be a tourist after reading this book. You'll be greater than a tourist!

-Alan Warner, Grand Rapids, USA

Thank you for a fantastic book.

-Don, Philadelphia, USA

Sabanovic Nihada

Great ideas for a port day.
-Mary Martin USA

Even though I only have three days to spend in San Miguel in an upcoming visit, I will use the author's suggestions to guide some of my time there. An easy read - with chapters named to guide me in directions I want to go.
-Robert Catapano, USA

Great insights from a local perspective! Useful information and a very good value!
-Sarah, USA

This series provides an in-depth experience through the eyes of a local. Reading these series will help you to travel the city in with confidence and it'll make your journey a unique one.
-Andrew Teoh, Ipoh, Malaysia

Tourists can get an amazing "insider scoop" about a lot of places from all over the world. While reading, you can feel how much love the writer put in it.
-Vanja Živković, Sremski Karlovci, Serbia

GREATER THAN A TOURIST – SARAJEVO BOSNIA AND HERZEGOVINA

50 Travel Tips from a Local

Sabanovic Nihada

Sabanovic Nihada

Greater Than a Tourist
Visit our website at www.GreaterThanaTourist.com

Lock Haven, PA

ISBN: 9781980430438

>TOURIST

50 TRAVEL TIPS FROM A LOCAL

Sabanovic Nihada

BOOK DESCRIPTION

Are you excited about planning your next trip?

Do you want to try something new?

Would you like some guidance from a local?

If you answered yes to any of these questions, then this Greater Than a Tourist book is for you.

Greater Than a Tourist- Sarajevo Bosnia and Herzegovina by Sabanovic Nihada offers the inside scoop on Sarajevo. Most travel books tell you how to travel like a tourist. Although there is nothing wrong with that, as part of the Greater Than a Tourist series, this book will give you travel tips from someone who has lived at your next travel destination.

In these pages, you will discover advice that will help you throughout your stay. This book will not tell you exact addresses or store hours but instead will give you excitement and knowledge from a local that you may not find in other smaller print travel books.

Travel like a local. Slow down, stay in one place, and get to know the people and the culture. By the time you finish this book, you will be eager and prepared to travel to your next destination.

Sabanovic Nihada

TABLE OF CONTENTS

DEDICATION

This book is dedicated to one man who stoled my heart in Sarajevo and made me to feel like most happy woman on planet. To Kemal, with love…

Sabanovic Nihada

ABOUT THE AUTHOR

My name is Sabanovic Nihada and I'm 31 years old. I was born in the most beautiful and the capital city of Bosnia and Herzegovina, In Sarajevo. I graduated in 2009 at the Faculty of Economics in Sarajevo. I like to travel and explore many countries, but I could never live anywhere else except in Sarajevo. My heart and soul belong to this city, and indeed, it's a city with a soul.

I work as an Administrative Assistant in one big Company and I am very satisfied with my work. In my free time I like reading, traveling and drawing. I am a positive person and very sociable and I am trying hard to be a good man and a good friend. Life is too short so that we could be unhappy, and I live every day as if it was the last one.

Sabanovic Nihada

HOW TO USE THIS BOOK

The Greater Than a Tourist book series was written by someone who has lived in an area for over three months. The goal of this book is to help travelers either dream or experience different locations by providing opinions from a local. The author has made suggestions based on their own experiences. Please do your own research before traveling to the area in case the suggested places are unavailable.

Sabanovic Nihada

FROM THE PUBLISHER

Traveling can be one of the most important parts of a person's life. The anticipation and memories that you have are some of the best. As a publisher of the Greater Than a Tourist book series, as well as the popular 50 Things to Know book series, we strive to help you learn about new places, spark your imagination, and inspire you. Wherever you are and whatever you do I wish you safe, fun, and inspiring travel.

Lisa Rusczyk Ed. D.
CZYK Publishing

Sabanovic Nihada

OUR STORY

Traveling is a passion of the "Greater than a Tourist" series creator. Lisa studied abroad in college, and for their honeymoon Lisa and her husband toured Europe. During her travels to Malta, an older man tried to give her some advice based on his own experience living on the island since he was a young boy. She was not sure if she should talk to the stranger but was interested in his advice. When traveling to some places she was wary to talk to locals because she was afraid that they weren't being genuine. Through her travels, Lisa learned how much locals had to share with tourists. Lisa created the "Greater Than a Tourist" book series to help connect people with locals. A topic that locals are very passionate about sharing.

Sabanovic Nihada

WELCOME TO
> TOURIST

Sabanovic Nihada

INTRODUCTION

When you go to Sarajevo, what you experience...is life
Mike Leight, English writter and director

Sarajevo is capital city of (the state of) Bosnia and Herzegovina. Sarajevo is situated in the area of Sarajevo plain, which is surrounded by mountains Bjelasnica and Igman from the Southwest, by Trebevic from the Southeast, middle-range mountains and inter-valley headlands (capes) on the North and Northwest.

On the following pages you will find 50 most beautiful things and places to visit in Sarajevo that I personally tried and enjoyed. Sarajevo is one of the most beautiful cities in Europe and is a city with a soul. Many songs have been written about Sarajevo and this city has been visited by many celebrities like Angelina Jolie.

Sarajevo is most beautiful in winter when it is covered by snow cover and when the laughter and screams of children playing are heard, while Ezan invites people to pray. Sarajevo is definitely a city that you need to visit and enjoy in a variety of foods that it offers, such as Cevapi - a traditional Bosnian dish.

Sabanovic Nihada

1. Visit Bascarsija

Bascarsija is an old Sarajevo place, and the historical and cultural center of the city. The place is visited by many tourists and it is inevitable because it is in the heart of Sarajevo. Bascarsija is a nice place to have a cup of coffee and talk with other people or friends.

In Bascarsija is Sebilj from which you have to drink water and it dominates in the city center. Bascarsija, within which the Old Orthodox Church is located, Gazi Husrev-beg's mosque, Medresa and Library, Clock Tower, Old Jewish Temple, Brus and Gazi-Husrev beg Bezistan, City Hall and many other sights is a monument under the protection of the state, cultural and historical the center of Sarajevo and an inevitable place.

2. Eat "Cevapi" at "Zeljo"

When you are in Sarajevo, you have to eat "cevapi" and the best are on Bascarsija (Sarajevo old town) in Zeljo. Atmosphere in Zeljo is very pleasant and they serve very decent grill. Cevapi are the national grilled speciality and one of the most famous Bosnian brands. Cevap is a small dumpling made of minced meat, mostly beef, with the addition of garlic, onion and different spices. Cevapi are fried on the grill and are traditionally served in somun or lepinja (type of homemade bread) dipped in grill souce with the addition with finely chopped onions. With cevapi you can usually drink jogurt because it taste delicious in this combination. In Zeljo are "must to" and you will be very pleased with food and service. Cevapi are amazing and you will feel like you are experiencing Bosnian history in one bite.

3. Relax at "Vidikovac" and enjoy at view on Sarajevo from height

Vidikovac is a caffe and restaurant that many visit to enjoy a respite for the soul, have a coffe break or to try the delicious specialities, all while enjoying a spectacular view of Sarajevo. Name Vidikovac means viewpint and that is exactly what you get – a drink with a magnificent panorama. Vidikovac is most popular on summer weekends and in summer nights. Many people from Sarajevo come here to drink coffe and to rest soul, and tourist also. When you come to Sarajevo don't forget to visit this place because u will fall in love in view, same moment when you come to Vidikovac. Vidikovac is best place to see whole town and it is specially beautiful to be here at night, so catch that view, so you can have memories your whole life.

4. Catch a Football Match at Grbavica

Grbavica Stadium is located in Grbavica, Sarajevo and it is the home of FK Zeljeznicar. It is also known as the Dolina Cupova – Valley of Cups. Here you can watch the best Sarajevo derby between two local football clubs FK Zeljeznicar and FK Sarajevo. If you are a football fan you have to visit these places and enjoy in best local match ever. For the fans of this club, this place have special value and often you can hear fans of these club how they support and cheer for their clubs by the streets of our city. Otherwise they are known as Manicas and Hordes of evil.

5. Attend to Basketball Match at Hall Mirza Delibasic

Mirza Delibasic hall is named after the greatest basketball player from Bosnia and Herzegovina who won the Euroleague Championship with Bosna Sarajevo in 1979. All home games basketball club Bosna plays in this hall and hall is located in the center of Sarajevo. If you are in Sarajevo during a basketball court, do not forget to visit this place and enjoy basketball. This hall carries the spirit of the famous generations who have won titles in numerous competitions and conveys the emotion of victory to young growths.

6. Take a drink at Hacienda Pub

The club and restaurant Hacienda, located in the heart of Bascarsija is a great place of any time of the day, where you can enjoy good time in electronic music and performances of bands as well as excellent Mexican food. Hacienda is one of the best places in Sarajevo and it is very popular if you want crazy night out. In the Hacienda you can drink super alcoholic cocktails but also many others drinks. Here you can hear electronic music and see best dancers while they perform their dance performance. So, Hacienda is definitely "must see".

7. Soak up some History at National Museum

The National Museum of Bosnia and Herzegovina is the oldest western-style cultural and scientific institution in the country. It was founded on February 1, 1888 and was first housed in a building next to the Sarajevo Cathedral. The museum allows visitors to take "a short walk" through Bosnian past, from the earliest tiimes all the way to the ethnology exhibit, whose interior captures the atmosphere of a traditional city house during the Ottoman period. The most valuable item in the Museum is the famous Sarajevo Haggadah, which the Separdic Jews brought to Sarajevo when they left Spain. There is also rich collection in the natural history section which covers both living and non-living worlds, including a skeleton of a bearded vuluture, a bird with a giant wingspan which used to fly in the skies above BiH, not that long ago. There is also a botanical garden in the central part of the complex, with more than 3000 types of plants, including some edemic varieties, so don't miss to see the National Museum.

8. Rent a bike and explore Spring of Bosna river - Vrelo Bosne

Spring of Bosnia river is a public park, featuring a spring of the river Bosna, at the foothills of the Mount Igman on the outskirts of Sarajevo. Vrelo Bosne is ideal place if u want to relax and enjoy in natural beauty of river Bosna and if you want to sit on a bench surrounded by swans that swim and birds who sing their summer songs. You can rent a bike and drive through the The Great Alley which leads to Vrelo Bosne. The Great Alley have more than 700 trees and it is ideal for walking and cycling or rolling and running. Many tourists come here to drink the water who springs from Mount Igman, and that is real natural watter without any additions and that makes this place more special. If you love nature this place will be ideal to visit when u come to Sarajevo.

9. Walk through Wilson's Promenade

Wilsons promenade is beautiful place in Sarajevo surrounded by nature. This is place if you want to be in natural and if you want to watch river Miljacka which flows through the city of Sarajevo. This is most popular place for loving couples and you can see many couples how they walk and how they are in love. If you are very romantic person than this place is for you. If you love to sit and read book or just be in nature this place is wonderful choice and you will not regret it. Wilsons promenade have many trees and it is best in summer or in autumn. So I suggest you to visit it, you will be fascinate how is calm and beautiful.

10. Watch the sunset that you will never forget from the Yellow   Fortress

If you were in Sarajevo and you didn't watch the sunset from the Yellom Fortress than you missed a lot in your life. Yellow Fortress is one of the most beautiful places in Sarajevo and especially when is our holy month Ramadan. During the month of Ramadan, this area is picked by locals waiting for the cannon to go off which marks the end of fasting that day, followed by some firewoks. If you cant make it for sunset, during the day is just as amazing, as it offers unrivalled views of the whole city. When you are in the Yellow Fortress you can see whole town especially old part of town Sarajevo. Please, don't miss this in your life if u ever come to my city. You will love it with your whole soul and heart.

11. Relax and swimm at Thermal Riviera

This complex of indoor and outdoor swimming pools with termal water and numerous animations offers entertainment and recreation for the whole family. Restaurant Tropic garden located within the Thermal Riviera offers specialities od domestic and internacionale couisine. The Thermal Riviera is located at the cery entrance to Sarajevo, known as Ilidza. Within the Thermal Riviera is a Hotel where you can stay while you are in Sarajevo visit. Prices for their services are low and services are top. People who work here are very kind and you will not regret if you visit these pools. Thermal Riviera offers cooling in warm Sarajevo days and those pools also include night swimming. So if u love to swim and relax, this is "must do".

12. Go for a picnic on Barice

Nine kilometers from Sarajevo is very interesting place for picnic called Barice. With beautiful nature, sprinkled with numerous trails ideal for walking and cycling, the offer of this resort also includes several catering facilities where visitors can enjoy delicious local specialties. If you like nature and you are in Sarajevo visit with your friends you have to visit this place for a picnic.

13. Taste burek in Forino

If you love to eat Bosnian specialties than this is definitely place for you. Forino is place where you can eat our traditional pie called "burek" and you can also taste many other pies like sirnica (cheese pie), zeljanica (spinach pie), potato pie, pumpkin pie etc. Burek is pie made of finely chopped or minced meat that is mixed with onion and spices and rolled into thin stretched layer of dough. In Bosnia and Herzegovina burek is often in the form of long rolled layer of dough bent into circle that suits round shallow casserole (tepsija) in which burek is baked. Burek used to be baked under the iron bell known as sac in the region. Forino is place where you can eat fantastic and fresh pies and you can find this place in our main street Titova. Visit and enjoy. Njammi

14. Walk down Titova Street

The most famous street in Sarajevo is Tito's street. The street used to change names by conquerors and dictators. If you ever visit Sarajevo you have to take walk thought this street because it extends through the heart of Sarajevo. When we celebrate some holidays like New Year 's Eve, this street is decorated with many light decorations. In this street there are various shops and boutiques and it is a famous Sarajevo promenade. So, please take a walk and enjoy in our shops and happy people.

15. Party at Face Club

If you love to party than this is place for you. Face club is night club where people from Sarajevo love to party. Club is at Wilson's promenade and it is best place to go for night out. Many celebrities from whole Bosnia and Hercegovina sing at this club and you will not regret at all if you visit this night club. Music you can listen at this club is usually fun and folk but also it is not strange to be electronic music also. The drinks served are alcoholic and non-alcoholic, and the duration of the service is until the early hours of the morning. For young people in Sarajevo this club is one of the best places to go on party, so, enjoy and have fun.

16. Smoke nargila at Dibek

Nargila is an instrument used for smoking aromatic tobacco and has become known at Sarajevo for the last few years. Best nargila you can find in Dibec, local caffe located in Bascarsija. This local caffe is always full of people and many tourist and people who work here are very kind and polite.

If you love to smoke Nargila than I suggest you Dibek. Dibek is especially popular place in the summer Sarajevo nights, as well as during the month Ramadan where people come to smoke nargila and to talk about everyday life. If you love to smoke nargila than go ahead in Dibek.

17. Go on dinner at Restaurant Prince Park – Park Princeva

Hidden at the very top of the Old city, restaurant "Park Princeva" has been always a place of the gathering for poets, bohemians, travelers and all the people who enshrine Sarajevo. Interior of the restaurant, carefully designed, as well as the natural surroundings of the very summer garden, can hardly leave you indifferent. This restaurant is very peaceful place if you want to eat some specialties of Bosnian kitchen while you are listening Bosnian songs in background. When you sit on terrace of this restaurant you have view on Old town Sarajevo and on Vijecnica and this is view which you will remember your whole life. If you ever come to arajevo this place is "must visit" definitely because you will be surprised how food is good and how service is fantastic. This place is place where you will feel like prince or princess, so it is "must visit".

18. Do shopping at SCC Center

Sarajevo City Center – SCC is comprised of four separate but at the same time complementary parts: a modern five-star hotel, commercial and office space, shopping center with entertainment complex and an underground parking garage to accommodate for the entire Center. If you love to shop clothes, to eats best fast Pizza in town or just to walk and enjoy to watch best world brands in fashion, sports and technology, than this is place for you. SCC is located in the Center of Sarajevo and it is surrounded by banks, Government buildings and dozens of international and local companies. The whole Center is covered with luminous advertisements and at night it is especially visible.

19. Go to scatting in Olympic Hall Zetra

Zetra Olympic Hall is an indoor multi-purpose arena in Sarajevo. Zetra Olympic Hall was constructed specifically for the 1984 Winter Olympics, hosted in Sarajevo, and was completed in 1982. Zetra is currently services as sporting arena, and it is also used for music concerts, fairs and conferences. If you come to Sarajevo and there is some concert than please go in Zetra and enjoy in music.

At Zetra you can skate every winter and on summer you can play tennis. Zetra is attraction for many young and old people and many tourists. Here you can play tennis, you can bowl, play pool and the price of these services is very cheap. Zetra is fantastic place for fun so please doesn't forget to visit it.

20. Taste a baklava at Local Baklava Shop

Baklava is a rich, sweet dessert pastry made of layers of filo filled with chopped nuts, sweetened and held together with syrup of honey. Baklava shop is an object in which every gourmet will find himself an appropriate traditional Bosnian-Turkish treat.

For baklava they say that it is a dessert worthy of the palates of the most powerful and riches. In Baklava Shop you can find several types and favors (walnuts, almonds, hazelnuts or pistachios).

Baklava shop is located in in the antique shop on the northern side of Bezistan, in center of Sarajevo. The interior is dominated with wooden and stone elements that ideally fit with old Bosnian motifs (pawn, seeds, etc.)

21. Take a photography at Resque Tunel

The Sarajevo War tunnel is the name for the tunnel built during the siege of Sarajevo in 1993. The tunnel is built under the airport runaway and connected two territories, which was held by ARBIH (Dobrinja and Butmir), so the tunnel was called "Tunel D-B".

The tunnel is about 720 meters long and about1.5 meters high, while in some parts is it was up to 1.8 high. During the war in Bosnia and Herzegovina many people are rescued and they survived thanks to this tunnel because on this way they could have food and clothes.

This tunnel during the war in Sarajevo was the strictest secret because food, clothes and cigarettes came through it. The Army of Republica Srpska found about this tunnel in 1994 and was ordered to break it but did not succeed. After the war in Bosnia and Herzegovina this tunnel become museum and a documentary " Tunnel – The Secret of the Siege of Sarajevo" was shot. You have to visit this museum because for people in Sarajevo this tunnel is the symbol of salvation.

22. Buy a souvenir at Gazi Husrev Bey's Bezistan

Bezistan is a covered market with small trading and crafts shops. They were built during the Ottoman in Bosnia and Herzegovina in the largest cities Sarajevo and Travnik. In Bezistan you can buy various Bosnian souvenirs that represent the history of Bosnia and Herzegovina. Bezistan is located in Sarajevo street known as Ferhadija just below Gazi Husrev Bey's mosque and it is visited by numerous tourists every year. In Bezistan you can buy something that will remind you of your stay in Sarajevo and on Bosnian culture.

23. Walk through Vijecnica

The Sarajevo Hall is a building in Sarajevo not so far from Bascarsija on Mustaj-pasa mejdan and is one of the most beautiful and most representative buildings in the Austro – Hungarian period built in a pseudo-Moorish style. In this style most buildings were left by

Austro-Hungarian authorities in Sarajevo and Vijecnica is trademark of that style.

Vijecnica is open for many tourist and it is perfect place to visit if you want to know more about Bosnian's history and to enjoy in old building.

On August 25, 1992 Vijecnica was set of fire and the Catalog of the National and University library of Bosnia and Herzegovina disappeared, about 80% of the library and documents that testify to the history of BiH. The interior of the hall was almost completely destroyed in a fire that followed the shelling.

The reconstruction of the City Hall began in 1996, and the ceremonial opening of the renovated Town Hall occurred on May 9, 2014, on the Day of Europe and the Day of Victory over Fascism.

24. Visit Kozja Cuprija – A bridge that represents two legends

In the Ottoman age, the Kozja Cuprija was a place where the emperors of the emperors were welcomed - Viziers. Every new Vizier would have made a welcome on the bridge. Before him, all the more visible people in Sarajevo would come out, and a common people would also gather because it was one of the most important events for the city. In honor of the new Vizier, some of the brave guys would jump from the river Miljacka, and he would give them money.

Jumping is an excitement for admiration, because the bridge is tall and Miljacka is shallow in that place.

The Kozja Cuprija is located several kilometers east of the old center of Sarajevo. The road on which the river was bordering was the famous Carigrad road, the path that, from the time of the Ottoman rule, from Sarajevo went towards the eastern parts of the Empire, all the way to Constantinople.

25. Enjoy in snow on Bjelasnica

A mountain that I believe everyone should visit is Bjelasnica. Bjelasnica held the men's alpine skiing events during the 1984 winter Olympics. The winter on Bjelasnica lasts from November to May. A particular attraction is the high snow heaps that may reach even several meters. Winters are particularly interesting exactly due to the snow covered mountain landscape, like a white, sun-bathed desert with nothing but the sky above it. Once you arrive on Bjelasnica, you are going to enjoy in snow and in skiing if you love to ski and if no, you can sit in many cafes and enjoy in hot chocolate or in vine (this is tradition when you come to this mountain). For the transportation of skiers to the top, two saucers are available, two anchors and one triple seat that travels 12 minutes to the top of the mountain. The best part of Bjelasnica is definitely the night skiing! Bjelasnica is equipped with spotlights for night skiing recreations. Do not miss your chance to sled down the trails where ski legends skied. Bjelasnica is located only 20 mins from Sarajevo and it is really nice place to visit and to have fun. Enjoy and don't forget to take a photograph.

26. Eat Meat at Restaurant Kulin Dvor

Highly qualified staff will provide you a pleasant stay and fulfill your wishes. The guarantee is a family tradition of 50 years.

Motel-restaurant "Kulin Dvor" is located in Semizovac on the main road M-18 Sarajevo – Tuzla, about 10 km from the center of Sarajevo.

Here you can eat the best specialties of national or international cuisine. I personally recommend lamb or veal because this place is recognizable exactly by these dishes.

While eating inside the music you enjoy is the traditional Bosnian music under the name Sevdalinka and if you decide to lunch or dinner on the terrace you enjoy in the sound of the river and the twitter of the bird. Great place for lunch or dinner and relaxation for the soul.

27. Visit Academy of Fine Arts

The Academy of Fine Arts, built to be the Evangelical Church, is considered one of the most beautiful buildings in Sarajevo.

The Academy of Fine Arts in Sarajevo was founded in 1972. It is a higher education institution with the longest tradition in BiH that provides education and training in the field of fine arts.

The Academy organized and participated in numerous artistic and scientific research projects, contributing to the Bosnian and Herzegovinian cultural and artistic realities.

The building was declared a cultural and historical monument and is on the list of protected objects of the Institute for the Protection of Cultural, Historical and Natural Heritage. If you want to enjoy in Bosnian history than you should visit this building which is located in the center of Sarajevo. In the evening hours, it is especially illuminated and the city gives beautiful colors.

28. Observe The Cathedral of the Jesus' sacred heart

The Cathedral of Jesus' Sacred Heart in Sarajevo is one of the most important religious buildings in Bosnia and Herzegovina and is the seat of the Archdiocese of Vrhbosna. It is located in the Old town in Sarajevo, in an attractive location led by the main city promenades. Since 1889, when blessed, the head of the spiritual life of the Catholic Regiment in Sarajevo. It is dedicated to the Heart of Jesus.

In front of this church there are numerous cafes where you can enjoy a variety of drinks and sweep the church

Due to its beauty, spiritual and historical significance, for over a century, the Cathedral attracted people of all religions from different parts of the world, especially during the tourist season. One of the most famous visitors was Pope John Paul II, who was visited in 1997

29. Take a photograph in front of Eternal fire - Vjecna vatra

Eternal fire is a monument to the liberators of Sarajevo in the Second World War, which was presented to the public on the occasion of the celebration of the first anniversary of the liberation of Sarajevo on April 6, 1946.

The memorial consists of a plaque with text printed in the colors of the flag of the former Yugoslavia - blue, white and red, in front of which there is a copper fireplace in the form of a laurel wreath, with an open and constantly ignited flame, which symbolizes an eternal vivid memory of the liberators of Sarajevo, but also the coat of arms of the former Yugoslavia.

When you come to Sarajevo you have to take photography in front of Eternal fire because this is almost tradition to all tourists. In front of Eternal fire you can see a person who heats their hands or what they stand and talk about everyday life. Also in the vicinity is a local caffe called "FIRE" where many Sarajevo personalities gather in coffee or cookies. It is located in the very heart of Sarajevo, in Tito's street and is an inevitable place to visit.

30. Eat Ice cream at Saraj

Traditionally famous and popular café-dessert, which with its kindness, attractiveness of the site and making the most beautiful cakes - takes the very top in the selection of such facilities in the city. Rrich services It is almost impossible to describe, the number of choices of all popular cakes, sweets made in the best possible masterful way. Every day, fresh and attractive almost all kinds of popular cakes, and delicacies. The building is located in the very center of Bascarsija - near the famous Sebilj and dates back to 1922.

The garden facing the center of Bascarsija is an unforgettable experience. In the embrace of the tradition and pigeons of the Bascarsija legend you can spend the most beautiful moments with coffee, cakes, ice cream or something else from a rich offer.

31. Shop along Bascarsija

In addition to the world brands that you can find in numerous shopping centers, Sarajevo also offers a large number of products from local manufacturers. Walk through the main shopping area, from Bascarsija, through the streets of Ferhadija and Tito, all the way to Marijin Dvor, and find the perfect gift for yourself or your dear ones.

Numerous open markets offer organic products, fruits, vegetables, spices and flowers. Do not miss to visit the picturesque market Markale in the Old Town. Twenty meters away there is a City Market where you can buy or just taste local dairy and meat products.

When purchasing a souvenir, you must not bypass Bascarsija, which has been the center of trade and crafts from the founding city. There you can find a large selection of precious handicrafts, jewelry, copper objects, oriental slippers and carpets, but also see the process of their manufacture, which is passed on from generation to generation by knee to knee. Bascarsija is full of practical and decorative engraved copper objects and you can find jewelry of specific design, such as belenzuka, as well as jewelry for various occasions from gold, silver and precious stones. In Bascarsija you can find large hand-made carpets and traditional clothes with unique Bosnian motifs.

32. Gasp at the panoramic view at Avaz Twist Tower

Avaz Twist Tower is the third avant-garde facility in which, in six years, Avaz Company has beautified Sarajevo. It is the highest business facility in the region and one of the most spectacular buildings in Europe. The Avaz Tower is among the ten most beautiful buildings in the world.

As such, the Avaz Twist Tower, along with Bascarsijaa, became an unavoidable detail on the tourist map of Sarajevo and all of BiH.

Namely, the tower's special attraction is at the top of the tower. One of the five lifts produced in Finland comes to the viewpoint, which goes up to five meters per second. From the top of the tower there is a magnificent view of the Sarajevo. In the summer season, the Avaz Twist Tower and the Avaz Twist Tower visit up to 10,000 tourists a month. So, I suggest you to be one of them and to enjoy in your view on Sarajevo.

33. Visit Gazi Husrev bey's Mosque

Gazi Husrev Bey's Mosque, or Bey's Mosque, as it is known locally, was built in the center of Bascarsija in 1530. Today, this mosque is rightly seen as the most important architectural monument from the time of Ottoman rule in Bosnia and Herzegovina.

This great and beautiful mosque is one of the most beautiful works of Islamic architecture in Bosnia and Herzegovina. The mosque is surrounded on all sides by the narrow streets of the old quarter, with tens and hundreds of shops, so that it is impossible to see it in its full beauty and greatness. However, when it enters its spacious yard, everything changes. An impressive building, full of peace, harmonious beauty and greatness, is in front of our eyes. This is not only the largest mosque ever built in this region but also the masterpiece of the Ottoman architecture. It's not unusual to see people, Muslims, doing prayer in the yard of this mosque, and the scene is fascinating and unforgettable. Ezan invites people to pray five times a day every day, and this mosque is covered with peace and warmth.

The main entrance to the mosque is exquisitely decorated with beautifully styled Arabic decor, ornament, gold and marble.

34. Visit Old Jewish Cemetery

The Old Jewish Cemetery, which is located in Kovacii, in the In the southwestern part of Sarajevo, is one of the largest Jewish sacral complexes in Europe. What makes this cemetery unique the world over is that the shape and motifs of the tombstones very closely resemble the medieval Bosnian stecci. This is due to the fact that the cemetery was founded in the vicinity of the medieval necropolis in Borak, where many stecci used to stand.

On the highest point of the cemetery grounds there is a white pyramid, a monument dedicated to the Jews who fell fighting during World War II and the victims of Fascism who perished in concentration camps. The oldest preserved tombstone at this cemetery belongs to the first Sarajevo rabbi. On the chest of his stećak he writes: Samuel Baruh, 1630-1650. The tombstone of the righteous.

35. Take a break at Roman bridge – Rimski most

The Roman Bridge is a building of striking appearance, built on Plandiste near Ilidža. This bridge is one of the 4 preserved old stone bridges in the area of Sarajevo.

It is called the Roman Bridge, but it was not built by the Romans. It was built by the Ottomans at the beginning of the 16th century. Turks also called him Cuprija at the source of the river Bosna. Today, very little is known about him, and he is under the protection of the National Commission of BiH.

It was made of late antique monuments and stone carvings. The length of the bridge is about 40 meters and the width is 4.5 meters. It consists of seven arches of which the central is the largest. He is a true representative of Ottoman architecture. If you want to enjoy in view on river Miljacka and in nature than you should visit this bridge.

This bridge is one of the most popular excursion places for people in Sarajevo.

36. Visit Svrzo's House

Svrzo's House represents the lifestyle of an urban Muslim family in the late 18th and throughout the 19th century. Svrzo's House is a typical example of the architecture of that period, with its division into the selamluk or public quarters and the haremluk or private, family quarters. It was purchased from the Svrzo family, refurbished and opened to the public in the 1960s. Following the siege of Sarajevo, the house was renovated and again opened to the public in 1997. In the 1960s the family sold the house to the Museum of the City of Sarajevo and it is now an annex of the Museum of Sarajevo. I suggest you to visit this house because you will enjoy in Bosnian History and this house you can find in Old town in Sarajevo.

Sabanovic Nihada

37. Watch pictures at Srebrenica Galery 11-07-95

The first Memorial gallery in Bosnia and Herzegovina - exhibition place aiming to preserve the memory on Srebrenica tragedy and 8372 persons who tragically lost their lives. Through a wide range of multimedia content - images, maps, audio and video materials, the Gallery aims to offer its visitors the documentary and artistic interpretation of the events that took place during July 1995 in Srebrenica. If you ask me, then this is the best gallery/museum in town. A must visit during your stay in Sarajevo. Unbelievably powerful exhibition that leaves you questioning everything. You can't be nothing else then wordless and lose the concept of time during your visit. The exhibition gives you this opportunity to share the pain of the victims' families and in all that sadness gives you a little bit of hope. The staff is very welcoming and knowledgeable.

38. See History at War Childhood Museum

The War Childhood Museum opened in Sarajevo in January 2017. The Museum's collection contains a number of personal belongings, stories, audio and video testimonies, photographs, letters, drawings and other documents offering valuable insight into the unique experience of growing up in wartime. The 2018 Council of Europe Museum Prize – one of the most prestigious awards in the museum industry – has been awarded to the War Childhood Museum under the European Museum of the Year scheme.

The museum is built on a simple but powerful concept of featuring one short story and a single item from many different survivors of the war. The stories are very humane and sometimes moving, and contrary to what you might expect they are not focused on the horror or bloody details. Small museum but a big impact. Great vision of sharing the lives and trauma of children who go through war.

39. Take photography at Latin bridge

Located in the Old Town, this bridge is one of the oldest bridges in the city. According to some records, first references to Latin bridge date from 1954. In Sarajevo people usually refer to it as Princip's Bridge (which was even its official name for some time), because it was precisely on its left side that Gavrilo Princip killed the Archduke Franz Ferdinand of Austria in 1914. This act triggered the beginning of the World War I. This is nice place to took photography because it is beautiful and somehow represents the Sarajevo in the full sense

40. Visit Olympic Bobsleigh Track

Once a proud feature of Sarajevo's 1984 Winter Olympic games, the bobsleigh track has since fallen into ruin after being the victim of military actions. Today, the track still stands as a favorite spot for local graffiti artists who have decorated whole swaths of the curving lane. The Sarajevo Bobsleigh Track is a literally concrete reminder of a more prosperous time. It is currently under re-construction for future bobsleigh competitions but official guided tours are still available.

A hike to the bobsleigh track is a hike through the agonizing recent history of Sarajevo. You can start in the Old City, and on the two hour trek to the top of Mount Trebevic you will pass by Muslim graveyards, by Serbian tombstones, and countless bullet and shell holes. The city still bears the scars of war to this day.

41. Drink beer at Pivnica HS

History, tradition and quality in one place best describe the unique catering facility in Sarajevo - HS brewery. It is located in the Center of Sarajevo, in the part of the Old Town of Bistrik, only a few meters from the Sarajevo Brewery, in a building that is a protected historical building. In addition to the Pivnica HS, there is the only brewing museum in BiH. Until the beginning of the aggression in Bosnia, this brewery was the favorite gathering place for poets, writers, actors, journalists and symbols of the Sarajevo Bohemian Mile. They offer a variety of dishes, from barbecue to meals to order from traditional Bosnian international and vegetarian cuisine, which will satisfy the biggest gourmets.

Of all the types of beers offered here, the light and dark Sarajevo beer is distinguished, which is produced only a few meters from the HS brewery, in the world-famous Sarajevo brewery, which has tradition since 1864.

42. Tako a close look at Sarajevo Old Clock Tower

Sarajevo's clock tower is 30 meters high and it is believed that it was built in the 16th century. The tower's clock is the only public clock in the world that keeps lunar time ("à la Turk"), to indicate the times for the daily prayers. According to this system, the new day starts at sunset, when the time is shown as 12:00. The tower's current clock mechanism was brought from London in 1875. It is situated next to Gazi Husrev-beg Mosque in the center of Bascarsija, Sarajevo.

43. Stay at the Hotel - Hecco deluxe

Hotel Hecco deluxe is located in the center of the city of Sarajevo. It has 15 luxuriously equipped apartments, which are equipped with the world's finest standards. On the 10th floor there is a restaurant offering an unforgettable view of Sarajevo's panorama. If you don't know where to stay while you are in Sarajevo than I suggest you this hotel. It is cheap and people who work in hotel are very kind and pleasant.

44. Visit the Sarajevo National Theater

The Sarajevo National Theater is the largest theater house in Bosnia and Herzegovina and one of the most significant in South East Europe. It was opened on November 17, 1921.

In the small rooms, the National Theater in Sarajevo, history has been saved, nine decades of work. Costumes, wearing the greatest acting, opera and ballet names of this area, keep their history - and they keep the careful hands of their employees.

Fundus Costumes of the National Theater in Sarajevo hosts thousands of costumes of drama, opera and ballet performances.

If you are a fan of performances, then I recommend that you visit the National Theater. The National Theater is the place where every Sarajevo Film Festival opens.

Sarajevo Film Festival is the most famous film festival in the region visited by Angelina Jolie.

45. Visit Moric's Han

Morić's han is a Gazi Husrev-bey's vakuf building that was erected in the heart of Sarajevo's Bascarsijaja at the end of the 16th or early 17th century. Moric han is the last preserved caravan-saraj on these premises. The caravan-range was a large building with an interior fully enclosed and fixed type for complete caravans.

In that time, Moric Han could take on a trolley of 300 passengers and 70 horses. If you like exploring history then I suggests you to visit this Han and enjoy in old Bosnian history

46. Take a photograph of the spot where East and West meets

There is a special spot in Sarajevo which everyone, whether they're a Sarajevan or a visitor, will say is the very spot where East and West collide, touch and connect. They don't just represent two distinct halves of the world, but two different civilizations. As you stand on this spot and turn to face west, the background of your photographs will show "Eastern" or Ottoman Sarajevo, with Gazi Husrev Bey's Bezistan, Slatko Ćoše (Sweet Corner), Aeroplan, Sarači Street....

And if you turn 180° to face east, you'll have the main walking area in the center of town, Ferhadija, behind you. This street is lined on both sides by structures that were built in a "Western style", during the period of Austro-Hungarian rule.

43

47. Stay at hotel Europe

Hotel Europe is located in the center of the city of Sarajevo, just a few steps from the main street and the old part of town, Bascarsija, famous for its architecture and small crafts from the Ottoman Empire.

Close to the hotel Europe there are almost all major historical and cultural sights. In addition to Jerusalem, Sarajevo is the only city in the world where the Catholic Cathedral, Orthodox Church, Mosque and Jewish Synagogue are located on a surface of less than one square kilometer and all around the Hotel Europe.

Hotel Europe, where the most important personalities from Europe and the world stayed, had been a silent witness to Sarajevo's history. The hotel was visited by distinguished statesmen and politicians, featuring corporate executives, film and television personalities, artists and athletes.

With the well-known "Vienna Cafee", a restaurant with top-of-the-range domestic and international culinary specialties and pastry "Mocart" with original pastries, the hotel Europe will refresh your spirit and make your stay in Sarajevo a unique experience that you will always remember with beautiful memories.

48. Visit Colosseum Club

Colosseum / Colosseum Club provides a unique gastronomic offer at its restaurant Arena, a relaxing atmosphere at Bachus bar and unforgettable parties on the slot machines or game tables. With its rich and unique program Colosseum Club has established itself as one of the most attractive clubs in the region. Try your luck on playing tables and playing machines. Magical light from playing machines turns Colosseum into an exciting fun avenue, unique in Sarajevo. Casino ensures intimate surrounding, and offers diversified entertainment that cleverly suits every desire. Colosseum is the only casino in Bosnia and Herzegovina where you can have fun at playing tables, playing machines and roulettes. Playing arena has 12 tables and it offers: American Roulette, Black Jack, Texas Hold'em Poker, Ultimate Texas Hold'em Poker and Hit draw progressive poker.

49. Give food to pigeons at Sebilj

Sebilj is one of the symbols of Sarajevo. It's in the middle of Bascarsija (sarajevos center) and easy to find it if you walk around Bascarsija. This fountain in the Bazaar is one of the symbols of the city of Sarajevo. The perfect place to meet up with friends and take photos, day and night. It's a small square but quite beautiful. Surrounded by pigeons.

In this place, pigeons are everywhere and the tradition is to feed them. For many this is the starting and/or meeting point to explore the old town. Sebilj (Fountain) has a long history, and its water was vital in the 1900's war. Sebilj (Fountain) is easily visible, and is well worth the time to visit and reflect.

50. Enjoy in vine at best wine shop "De Broto"

The "House of Wine De Broto" winery has become a place of gathering lovers of top-level wines from Herzegovina, mediteran and good entertainment in a short time. In this city wine cellar at any time of the day or night you can enjoy the tastes of various wines of the famous Citluk Winery and it is located in Center of Sarajevo. In the wine house "House of Wine De Broto", two exceptional wines are offered with special pleasure: Cabernet Sauvignon, an intense ruby-red wine, and Tvrtko, top quality wine is shining with golden yellow color.

>TOURIST

Sabanovic Nihada

TOP REASONS TO BOOK THIS TRIP

☐ **A place of rich history** - In Sarajevo, you will find the traces of Neolithic Butmir civilization, Illyrians, Romans, Slavs, the legacy of the medieval Bosnian kingdom, the Ottoman and Austro-Hungarian Empire, the Kingdom and the Socialist Republic of Yugoslavia ...Sarajevo is a place of rich history and has to tell its visitors a lot of fascinating stories.

☐ **Delicious and organic food** - The morning in Sarajevo starts with a traditional Bosnian coffee, which is served in small copper bowls. With lunch there is a selection of wines grown in vineyards of Herzegovina from authentic grape varieties Zilavka and Blatina, and evening entertainment is almost unimaginable without Sarajevo beer, obtained from the city's brewery, which has been operating since 1888. Traditional food is very tasty and organic. Cevabdzinice offer chefs - grilled meat rolls served in a flat bread (somun), ascensor a wide selection of traditional cooked dishes, and in buregdzinice you can choose some Bosnian pie.

☐ **Beautiful nature** - With all the advantages that a major city can offer to a visitor, in Sarajevo you will be able to find in just 10 minutes of driving, or less than an hour of walking, completely outside the urban milieu, in a beautiful and unspoiled nature, surrounded by greenery and shade of trees and the freshness of the rivers and streams, where the aroma of flowers and beautiful bird voting will sound.In

Sabanovic Nihada

winter, all of this has been united, and ski resorts in which the XIV Winter Games have been held are only half an hour away from the city, so you can find yourself in a beautiful mountain house, where you will enjoy the winter spell with the cracking fire in the fireplace.

The world is a book and those who do not travel read only a page.
Saint Augustine

> TOURIST
GREATER THAN A TOURIST

Visit GreaterThanATourist.com:

http://GreaterThanATourist.com

Sign up for the Greater Than a Tourist Newsletter:

http://eepurl.com/cxspyf

Follow us on Facebook:

https://www.facebook.com/GreaterThanATourist

Follow us on Pinterest:

http://pinterest.com/GreaterThanATourist

Follow us on Instagram:

http://Instagram.com/GreaterThanATourist

Follow on Twitter:

http://twitter.com/ThanaTourist

Sabanovic Nihada

> TOURIST
GREATER THAN A TOURIST

Please leave your honest review of this book on Amazon and Goodreads. Thank you. We appreciate your positive and constructive feedback. Thank you.

Sabanovic Nihada

NOTES

Printed in Great Britain
by Amazon

43780646R00040